It Wasn't Love

(It Was You)

It Wasn’t Love
(It Was You)

Ben Szuhaj

Radix Press
2015

Ben Szuhaj

It Wasn't Love

First Printing: 2015

ISBN 978-1-4951-6099-8

Radix Press
525 Burnham Road
Philadelphia, PA, 19119

https://www.facebook.com/benszuhajwritesbooks

Ordering Information:
Special discounts are available on quantity purchases by corporations, associations, educators, and others. For details, contact the publisher at the above listed address.

U.S. trade bookstores and wholesalers: Please contact Radix Press Tel: (215) 356-7323 or email Benjamin.J.Szuhaj.19@Dartmouth.edu.

Dedication

For Zoe,
My inspiration.

And everything else.

Ben Szuhaj

Acknowledgements

I would specifically like to thank my parents, who have helped me to follow my dreams, as well as the teachers, friends, and loved ones who have given me a reason to dream in the first place.

She began as a question mark.

Ben Szuhaj

That I could not approach.

I didn't know what questions to ask.

So I followed her to a party, where there were
questions to borrow.

Ben Szuhaj

I asked her a silly one.

She laughed like Spring.

But her smile faded quickly, flattening, the way water becomes still after the skipping of a stone. *She has questions about me,* I thought, realizing her apprehension.

Apprehensions... I thought.

She had apprehensions.

So I decided to hand myself to her, and by doing so, dispel them.

Ben Szuhaj

I asked her to a dance.

We went.

After the dance,

we fell asleep.

Life continued in the meantime.

+

She felt a basic curiosity for me.

More went on.

But we found ourselves lying next to one another one night some time later in the soft light of a single candle and I looked at her and she looked at me and it was just the way I’d always wished to be looked at.

I fell in love.

Ben Szuhaj

Same with her.

Love is the accidental discovery of happiness from nothing.

Later on, I'd start to believe that nothing was just the circumstance, and that we were the ones who filled it with meaning.

It Wasn’t Love

One day, we were walking. Past us there was a tall church steeple.
I pointed to the church steeple and said, “See that steeple?”
She nodded.

“Well,” I got close to her ear and whispered,

“To be with you
I would
Take everything I own
and
Toss it from that steeple
and
Turn to you
and walk away
before I heard it bounce.”

Ben Szuhaj

Perhaps finding love is what makes the nothing we come from okay.

We went into the city and found a spot near the west end of a park. The sidewalk, where I stood, was busy. She climbed up onto the rock wall that ran along the sidewalk and remained there, standing, for about a minute. Then she jumped. What I remember

is

catching her under the arms,

and

spinning around to face front,

the edges of her dress spinning with us.

She disembarked, feet meeting the sidewalk. I could hear the laughter in her silent smile. I could feel it in the way she scrunched up the corners of her eyes when she did. Someday, I imagined, she would have smile lines there. I didn't know if that bothered her, but it certainly didn't bother me. Those lines would hold memories, a result of days like this. And her laugh would still sound like Spring.

We spent the whole of the day doing that, repeatedly, without rest. We could, as we had two things:

Youth

&

A desire to show the world what happiness looked like.

Ben Szuhaj

She heals the broken parts of me.

It Wasn't Love

We went to the beach when the day had grown old. It was a fine day, salty and cool. There was a breeze.

We walked to the water line.

It was late. We got down onto our stomachs, laying flat. The sand was still warm. Looking out over the ocean, we could see the lower lip of the sun as it touched the horizon. It sank faster than I expected: gone in a minute, leaving its mark in the sky the way a fire gone-out leaves embers.

"Quick!" I rose to my feet, extending a hand to her.
"What! What is it?" Her excitement was infectious.
"Here," I hoisted her up, all the way, until she sat on my shoulders.

There was the sound of my brief exertion, and then nothing besides the waves.

"Wow." I felt it whispered from above my head.
I smiled to myself, squeezed her ankle. I did not speak.
I knew what was happening. I couldn't see it with my own eyes.
But
that didn't matter.

She got to see it:
The sunset, again.

That was enough for me.

Ben Szuhaj

Experience came stronger in two.

We shared a single memory:
It was the time capsule of our young days, our remembrance, into which we poured like the breaking of a dam the unbridled record of each other's existence.

Love is becoming each other’s consequences.

Ben Szuhaj

After the sun went down:
It was night.

People ought to be wildly unburdened and together
at irrational hours more often.

She sent me a letter:

"You are the love of my life."

I wrote her one back:

"You are the Life of my Love."

I wrote her a second.

You are the love of my life. The color in my world. You are the color, like spindles of the sun descending over dusky water, bright on the shifting surface, that so enthralls my eye. You capture my attention in gold.

You speak and listen intelligently. You are patient. You are patient with me when I cannot speak any better than a child because I have fallen somewhere deep into your beauty.

You possess a constant, evident radiance that allows me to think only of you, and what you are; and whether the world is fire or ice or falling apart I do not care as long as you are in it.
With me.

You are the love of my life. You are honest, noble, kind, and pure. You extend my thinking, clarify my ideas, and strengthen my beliefs. You empower, delight, soothe, and comfort me. You are the prettiest, kindest, most resilient, adventurous and thoughtful person I have ever known, will ever know, and even that's an understatement.

In short, you love me, and that is something to be cherished.

She sent me a second letter:

"I want to do everything on Earth with you."

Ben Szuhaj

We went out one night because we could.

"Streetlight looks good on you," I told her.

"You know," she began to respond, "People always say falling in love is amazing. I don't think it is. I don't even think it's good."

I was very still.

"I think falling in love with the right person is amazing."
She stopped again, gathering herself.

"It wasn't falling in love that made me happy. It was you."

I understood.

Ben Szuhaj

It had taken thousands of happy minutes, but I had found it:

The question I had been searching for since the beginning.

I knew exactly what I wanted.

I wanted an eternity of happy minutes.

Ben Szuhaj

I asked her for them.

“?”

She smiled, her face blossoming in surprise. Shaking, she threw her arms around my shoulders. Her slender arms were stronger than I had thought. I felt her happy sobs on my wet neck, the rise and fall of her chest pressed to mine.

She squeezed a ball of my shirt in her fist and whispered, her voice tightening with her hand:

"Yes."

"I do."

About the Author

Ben Szuhaj, born in 1996, is a student and distance runner at Dartmouth College. He won the Philadelphia Young Playwright's Festival and was afforded the privilege of seeing his play performed. He enjoys state parks, travel, good coffee, bad coffee, laughter, rap music, and unraveling metaphors. Most of all, he enjoys the company of others. Currently, he is working on multiple projects, including a novel, which he hopes to prepare for release in the fall of 2015.

Made in the USA
Middletown, DE
18 October 2021

50572687R00031